WYOMING

by William David Thomas

GARETH**STEVENS**

GS

PUBLISHING

A Member of the WRC Media Family of Companies

Please visit our web site at: www.garethstevens.com
For a free color catalog describing Gareth Stevens Publishing's
list of high-quality books and multimedia programs, call
1-800-542-2595 (USA) or 1-800-387-3178 (Canada).
Gareth Stevens Publishing's fax: (877) 542-2596.

Library of Congress Cataloging-in-Publication Data

Thomas, William, 1947-
    Wyoming / William David Thomas.
        p. cm. — (Portraits of the states)
    Includes bibliographical references and index.
    ISBN-10: 0-8368-4712-1   ISBN-13: 978-0-8368-4712-3 (lib. bdg.)
    ISBN-10: 0-8368-4729-6   ISBN-13: 978-0-8368-4729-1 (softcover)
    1. Wyoming—Juvenile literature. I. Title. II. Series.
    F761.3.T47   2007
    978.7—dc22   2006006743

Updated edition reprinted in 2007. First published in 2007 by
Gareth Stevens Publishing
A Weekly Reader Company
1 Reader's Digest Rd.
Pleasantville, NY 10570-7000 USA

Copyright © 2007 by Gareth Stevens, Inc.

Editorial direction: Mark J. Sachner
Project manager: Jonatha A. Brown
Editor: Catherine Gardner
Art direction and design: Tammy West
Picture research: Diane Laska-Swanke
Indexer: Walter Kronenberg
Production: Jessica Morris and Robert Kraus

Picture credits: Cover, © Eugene G. Schulz; p. 4 © Swift/Vanuga Images/CORBIS;
p. 5 © Howie Garber/Idaho Stock Images; p. 6 © CORBIS; p. 7 © MPI/Getty Images;
p. 9 © North Wind Picture Archives; p. 10 © Stock Montage/Getty Images; p. 12
© George Steinmetz/CORBIS; p. 15 © Robert Nickelsberg/Getty Images; p. 16
© Kevin R. Morris/CORBIS; pp. 18, 26 © Dennis MacDonald/PhotoEdit; pp. 20,
22, 24, 27 © John Elk III; p. 25 © AP Images; p. 28 © Robert Y. Ono/CORBIS;
p. 29 © Dave G. Houser/Post-Houserstock/CORBIS

Printed in the United States of America

2 3 4 5 6 7 8 9 10 09 08 07

CONTENTS

Words that are defined in the Glossary appear
in **bold** the first time they are used in the text.

On the Cover: Wyoming's Grand Teton National Park, known for its
beautiful, snow-capped mountains, is home to many varieties of wildlife.

Introduction

Come to Wyoming! This state has tall mountains and thick pine forests. It also has wide plains with few trees. You may see buffalo on these plains, and you will surely see cattle ranches. After all, Wyoming is called the Cowboy State. It is also called the Equality State. It was the first place in the United States where women could vote.

Wyoming is a big place that has few people. Here you can visit great national parks. You can ski in the mountains. On some ranches, you can live like a cowboy for a week. So come to Wyoming. You may run into ranchers, park rangers, oil workers, and miners. Come and meet them! See their big, wide-open state.

Cowboys still work on many ranches in Wyoming. These cowboys are riding the range at a guest ranch in Laramie.

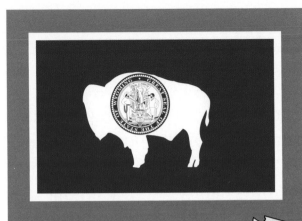

The state flag of Wyoming.

WYOMING FACTS

- Became the 44th U.S. State: July 10, 1890
- Population (2006): 515,004
- Capital: Cheyenne
- Biggest Cities: Cheyenne, Casper, Laramie, Gillette
- Size: 97,100 square miles (251,489 square kilometers)
- Nicknames: the Cowboy State, the Equality State
- State Tree: Plains cottonwood
- State Flower: Indian paintbrush
- State Mammal: American bison
- State Bird: Western meadowlark

History

Five hundred years ago, many Native Americans lived on Wyoming's plains. The Arapaho, Cheyenne, Shoshone, and Sioux were some of the tribes that lived here. They traveled from place to place, following herds of buffalo. These people lived in small tents, called teepees. The teepees were made from buffalo skins.

People of the Shoshone tribe listen to their chief in 1892. By this time, the Shoshone were living on a reservation in Wyoming.

Mountain Men

White fur traders may have visited this area in the 1740s. The first known white man here was François Antoine Larocque. He came in 1805 and traded furs with the Native Americans. An American named John Colter explored parts of Wyoming in 1807.

In the 1820s, trappers came to the area looking for beaver. Beaver furs were worth a lot of money. These trappers were called "mountain men." Most of the time, mountain men and Native Americans got along. They traded furs

Fort Laramie was built on the Laramie River near the North Platte River. It was a trading post first and then an army fort. In the mid-1800s, it became an important stop along the Oregon Trail.

and other goods with each other. The first trading post was built in 1834. Later, it became Fort Laramie. It was the first **permanent** white settlement in the area.

On the Way West

More Americans began coming west in the 1840s. Some dreamed of finding gold. Others wanted land. In the mid-1800s, thousands of people traveled on wagon routes across the state. One of the routes was the famous Oregon Trail. At first, the

IN WYOMING'S HISTORY

Colter's Hell

John Colter was a mountain man. He visited what is now Wyoming in 1807. In one area, Colter saw pools of water that were hot, even in winter. He saw puddles of boiling mud. He watched hot water shoot into the air from holes in the ground. When he told people about it, no one believed him. They made jokes and called the area "Colter's Hell." In 1871, some mapmakers visited the area. They made pictures of the wonders there. The land was set aside as a park in 1872. It became Yellowstone, the first U.S. national park.

FUN FACTS

The Wyoming Jackalope

Visitors to Wyoming may see pictures and hear stories about jackalopes. The town of Douglas has a statue of a jackalope. The animal has long ears like a jackrabbit. It has horns like an antelope or an elk. But there is no such animal as a jackalope. It is just one way that folks in Wyoming have fun with visitors to their state.

Native Americans let the whites cross their land. But the **pioneers** killed or scared away animals that the tribes hunted for food. They also brought diseases that killed many Native people. When fighting broke out between Natives and whites, soldiers were sent to Wyoming. The Army built forts there.

Trouble over the Trail

In the early 1860s, gold was found in Montana. Lots of miners headed for Montana on the Bozeman Trail. This trail went through Wyoming. The Army built forts along the trail. The Sioux who lived in the area fought the miners and soldiers. Finally, the Army agreed to close its forts, and the Sioux agreed to move to a **reservation**.

The Railroad

In 1867, the Union Pacific Railroad reached Wyoming. Men building the railroad lived in big tent camps. Stores and restaurants were built in these camps. The camps grew into Cheyenne, Laramie, and other towns.

At first, ranchers brought cattle from Texas to help feed the railroad workers. Soon, ranchers began to raise cattle in Wyoming. It became a big business in the state.

Mining also became an important business. People had known for years that there was coal in Wyoming. Train engines used coal as fuel, so mines were opened to supply it.

This picture shows the town of Sherman in 1869. Many towns sprang up along newly laid railroad tracks in the late 1860s.

Famous People of Wyoming

Red Cloud

Born: 1822, near North Platte, Nebraska

Died: December 10, 1909, Pine Ridge Agency, South Dakota

Red Cloud was a leader of the Sioux tribe. In 1866, he led his people in a fight to keep whites from using the Bozeman Trail. After two years of fighting, Red Cloud won. He is known as the only Native American to win a war with the United States.

Equality for Women

The Wyoming **Territory** was set up in 1868. The next year, Wyoming made history. Its **legislature** gave women the right to vote. At that time, women were not allowed to vote anywhere else in the world. Wyoming women also could be elected to office and serve on juries.

Coal Strikes and Gunmen

The territory grew. Problems grew, too. In 1875, the coal miners went on **strike**. They wanted more money and a safer place to work. But the mine owners simply hired new workers from China. This made the miners angry. They fought with the new workers. Some people were hurt or killed in the fights.

IN WYOMING'S HISTORY

Buffalo Bill and the Wild West
William Cody was a scout for the army and a hunter. In 1883, Cody started a traveling show. He called it Buffalo Bill's Wild West. It showed what life on the frontier was like. It featured shows of horseback riding, a pretend stagecoach robbery, and fancy shooting. Cody's show was a big hit in the United States and in Europe. Later, Cody bought a ranch in Wyoming. The town of Cody is named for him.

In 1869, women in the Wyoming Territory were given the right to vote. Here, women are lining up to cast their votes in Cheyenne.

Ranchers had trouble, too. Small ranch owners put up fences. Some began raising sheep. The big cattle ranch owners did not want fences or sheep. In 1892, fighting began among cattlemen, sheepmen, and small ranch owners. It was called the Johnson County War. It went on for nearly twenty years.

FUN FACTS

Women First!

In 1869, Wyoming's women were the first to get the right to vote. The next year, the state had the nation's first female judge. The first woman to win a statewide election won in Wyoming in 1894. And in 1925, this state became the first to elect a female governor.

Statehood and Beyond

On July 10, 1890, Wyoming became the forty-fourth U.S. state. Women in the state kept their right to vote. In 1912, a large amount of oil was found near Casper. The state became a big producer of both oil and coal.

Life in Wyoming changed during the 1920s. **Droughts** caused crops and cattle to die. Miners' strikes hurt the coal business. Then, prices for goods and crops fell all over the country as the **Great Depression** began. Many businesses in the state were forced to close.

The United States entered World War II in 1941. Wyoming's coal, oil, lumber, and cattle were needed for the war. Ranchers and miners went back to work. After the war, the

IN WYOMING'S HISTORY

Heart Mountain

In 1941, the United States went to war against Japan. People did not trust Japanese Americans living in the United States. Thousands of Japanese Americans were forced to go to special camps. One of these was the Heart Mountain Center, in Wyoming. Soldiers guarded the camp. Barbed wire surrounded it. In the camp, people lived in crowded shacks with little heat and no running water. Many stayed in the camps for three years. Years later, the U.S. government apologized to all Japanese Americans.

Black Thunder is a big coal mine in Wyoming. In 2004, more coal came from Black Thunder than from any other mine in the nation.

government built a big Air Force base near Cheyenne. This brought people and jobs to the state. Then, lots of uranium was found. New uranium mines created even more jobs.

Today, Wyoming has cattle ranches, coal mines, and oil wells. It has lots of empty space, too. And most folks in the state like it that way.

FUN FACTS

Young Drivers

In Wyoming, children of any age can drive tractors or trucks on their ranches or farms. Some can get licenses to drive to school when they are just fourteen years old!

★ ★ ★ Time Line ★ ★ ★

1807	American John Colter explores the Yellowstone region.
1834	first permanent trading post is built in Wyoming.
1840s-'50s	Thousands of pioneers cross Wyoming on their way west.
1863-1868	Native Americans battle miners and soldiers along the Bozeman Trail.
1867	The Union Pacific Railroad reaches Wyoming.
1868	The Territory of Wyoming is formed.
1869	Wyoming women get the right to vote and hold office.
1872	Yellowstone becomes the world's first national park.
1890	Wyoming becomes the forty-fourth U.S. state.
1892	The Johnson County War begins between cattle ranchers and sheep ranchers.
1912	Lots of oil is found near Casper.
1951	Uranium is found in Wyoming.
2000	Richard B. Cheney, who grew up in Casper, is elected vice president of the United States. He is reelected in 2004.

People

Wyoming has fewer people than any other state in the United States. Lots of people come to Wyoming, but not many stay.

Just Passing Through

In the mid-1800s, wagon trains brought thousands of pioneers to Wyoming. Most of them went on to Oregon or California. Mining brought people to the state, too. Then, the prices for oil, gas, and coal fell. Many miners and oil workers lost their jobs

Hispanics

This chart shows the different racial backgrounds of people who live in Wyoming. In the 2000 U.S. Census, 6.4 percent of the people in Wyoming called themselves Latino or Hispanic. Most of them or their relatives came from places where Spanish is spoken. Hispanics do not appear on this chart because they may come from any racial background.

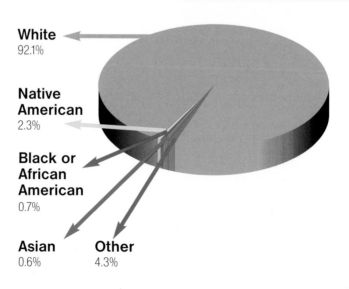

The People of Wyoming

Total Population 515,004

White
92.1%

Native American
2.3%

Black or African American
0.7%

Asian
0.6%

Other
4.3%

Percentages are based on the 2000 Census.

so they moved away. Today, millions of tourists come to the state every year. After a visit, they go home.

Cities and Towns

About two-thirds of the people in Wyoming live in cities and towns. Most cities are in the southeastern part of the state. All of the cities are small. Some towns are just a few buildings along a highway. Wyoming has ghost towns, too. They are small towns that are empty because all of the people have moved away.

Natives and Immigrants

More than eleven thousand Native Americans live in Wyoming. More than half of them live on the Wind River Indian Reservation. It is the only reservation in the state.

Non-Natives first came to Wyoming in the early 1800s. Most of them were white people from the East Coast. Chinese workers came in the

Native Americans in Wyoming are proud of their history and culture. Here, a group of Natives perform the Round Dance at a powwow in the city of Cody.

1860s to build the railroad. Later, other **immigrants** came from Europe. These people came from Britain, Germany, Russia, Ireland, and other countries.

Today, most people who move to Wyoming come from other U.S. states. A few come from Mexico.

Religion and Education

In Wyoming, most people of faith belong to a Protestant religion. The state is home to many different Protestant churches. Roman Catholic and Mormon churches are found in the state, as well.

The state's first school started at Fort Laramie in 1852. In 1869, the territory of Wyoming set up a tax to help pay for schools.

Today, Wyoming spends lots of money for each of its students. It spends more than any state except Alaska. Many schools are small, and the children who attend them live far apart. To get to school, some students have to travel 75 miles (121 km) each way. Some of the state's smallest towns have schools with just one teacher. In these schools, the same person teaches all of the classes, from kindergarten through eighth grade.

Wyoming's only four-year college is the University of Wyoming. It was founded in 1886. Today, more than eleven thousand students go to the **campus** in Laramie each year. Wyoming also has a number of two-year colleges around the state.

Famous People of Wyoming

Esther Hobart Morris

Born: August 8, 1814, Tioga County, New York

Died: April 2, 1902, Cheyenne, Wyoming

Esther Morris came to Wyoming with her husband, looking for gold. She worked to pass a law that let women vote. In 1869, women in Wyoming got the right to vote and hold office. The next year, Morris was made a justice of the peace. She was the first female judge in the United States. On her first day, her husband caused trouble in the court. Morris said he had to pay a fine. When he refused to pay Morris sent him to jail! A lawyer said, "She showed no mercy, but her decisions were always fair."

The Land

People say that Wyoming is "high and dry." The land in this state is quite high, compared to other states. The mountains get some rain and lots of snow, but the rest of the state is very dry. Summers are short in Wyoming, and winters are long and very cold.

Plains, Mountains, and Basins

Wyoming has three main land areas. They are the **Great Plains**, Rocky Mountains, and Basin areas. Each is very different from the others.

Eastern Wyoming is part of the Great Plains. This is a huge area of rolling land. It covers much of the middle of the United States. In

Devils Tower rises high above the plains in eastern Wyoming.

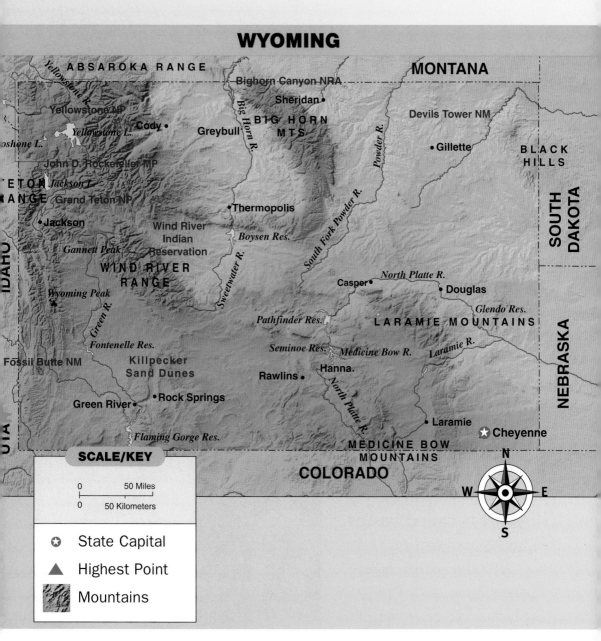

WYOMING

MONTANA

ABSAROKA RANGE

Bighorn Canyon NRA

Yellowstone R.

Sheridan

Yellowstone NP

Devils Tower NM

Yellowstone L.

Cody

Greybull

BIG HORN MTS

Big Horn R.

Powder R.

Gillette

BLACK HILLS

oshone L.

John D. Rockefeller MP

SOUTH DAKOTA

TETON RANGE

Jackson L.

Grand Teton NP

Thermopolis

South Fork Powder R.

Jackson

Wind River Indian Reservation

Boysen Res.

IDAHO

Gannett Peak

WIND RIVER RANGE

Sweetwater R.

North Platte R.

Casper

Douglas

Wyoming Peak

Green R.

Pathfinder Res.

LARAMIE MOUNTAINS

Glendo Res.

Fontenelle Res.

Seminoe Res.

Medicine Bow R.

Laramie R.

Fossil Butte NM

Killpecker Sand Dunes

Hanna.

NEBRASKA

Rawlins

North Platte R.

Green River

Rock Springs

Laramie

Cheyenne

Flaming Gorge Res.

MEDICINE BOW MOUNTAINS

COLORADO

SCALE/KEY

0 — 50 Miles

0 — 50 Kilometers

⊙ State Capital

▲ Highest Point

Mountains

N
W — E
S

Wyoming, the plains mainly are grassland. Most of the state's cattle are raised here.

Several ranges of the Rocky Mountains spread across Wyoming. The Teton Range is in the far western part of the state. The Wind River Range runs southeast from the Tetons. The state's highest mountain is in this range. Gannett Peak rises 13,804 feet (4,207 meters). The Big Horn Mountains are in the north-central part of the state. In the southeast are the Laramie Mountains.

The northeastern corner of Wyoming includes part of the Black Hills. They are small mountains, covered with dark pine trees. They are **sacred** land for many Native Americans.

Between the mountains in south-central Wyoming are low areas called basins. The basin land is mostly flat and grassy, with few trees. Most of it is very dry. The Killpecker Sand Dunes

Major Rivers
Green River 730 miles (1,175 km) long
North Platte River 680 miles (1,094 km) long
Yellowstone River 671 miles (1,080 km) long

are near one of the basins. These big hills of sand are some of the largest dunes in the world.

Yellowstone National Park is in the western mountains. Here, water plunges over Yellowstone Falls.

Water

Wyoming is the starting point for three great river systems. The Missouri, the Colorado, and the Columbia Rivers start in the mountains of Wyoming. Rushing water has made deep canyons and high waterfalls in parts of the state. The Lower Falls in Yellowstone Park reach 308 feet (94 m) high. In the mountains are hundreds of bright blue and green lakes.

Plants and Animals

Some of the biggest animals in North America can be found in Wyoming. Bighorn sheep live in the mountains. The largest herd of buffalo in the United States roams the state's plains. Grizzly bears live in the forests. Wyoming also is home to bald eagles, elk, and wolves.

Salmon, trout, bass, and catfish swim in Wyoming's

FUN FACTS

That's Fast!

When someone runs fast, people often say that person "runs like a deer." They really should say the person "runs like a pronghorn." These animals live on Wyoming's plains. Pronghorns can run 60 miles (97 km) per hour. The cheetah is the only animal that can run faster.

lakes and rivers. They share the water with ducks, swans, and pelicans.

Most of Wyoming's forests are in the mountains. The the plains cottonwood is the state tree. It grows on the eastern plains. Many types of grasses grow in this part of the state. In spring and summer, wildflowers bloom. Goldenrod, forget-me-nots, and buttercups grow here. The state flower, the Indian paintbrush, grows here, too.

Economy

The U.S. government owns half of the land in Wyoming. The government controls the way this land can be used.

In Wyoming, products from the land are very important. They bring in more money than any other kind of business in this state. Manufacturing is not as important. Wyoming has fewer factories than most other states.

Oil and Coal

This state is one of the biggest producers of oil and natural gas in the nation. It is the nation's biggest producer of coal. A coal-burning power plant is the tallest building in Wyoming. It makes more

Cattle still roam over large areas of land in Wyoming. Cattle ranching is big business in this state.

electricity than the people in the state need. Wyoming sells some of the electricity it makes to other states.

Cattle and Sheep

The biggest farm product in the state is cattle. Sheep and wool also are important. On some ranches, hay and grain are grown for the animals. But most of the land is too dry for crops. Some logging is done in the mountains.

Tourism

Each summer, thousands of tourists visit Yellowstone and Grand Teton National Parks. Tourists visit dude ranches, too. There, they can ride horses and see ranch hands at work. In winter, skiers head for the mountains. All of these places need workers to help the tourists. They make jobs for many people.

How Money Is Made in Wyoming

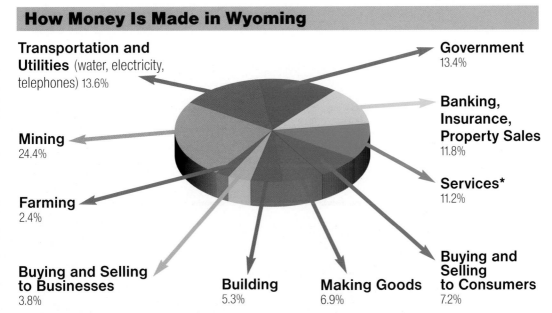

Transportation and Utilities (water, electricity, telephones) 13.6%

Mining 24.4%

Farming 2.4%

Buying and Selling to Businesses 3.8%

Building 5.3%

Making Goods 6.9%

Government 13.4%

Banking, Insurance, Property Sales 11.8%

Services* 11.2%

Buying and Selling to Consumers 7.2%

* Services include jobs in hotels, restaurants, auto repair, medicine, teaching, and entertainment.

Government

Wyoming's state government meets in the capital city, Cheyenne. Like the government of the United States, it has three parts, or branches.

Executive Branch

The executive branch carries out the laws of the state. The governor leads this branch. The secretary of state is the next highest official.

Legislative Branch

The legislative branch makes the laws for the state. It has two parts. They are

The state capitol building is in Cheyenne. The leaders of the state government meet here.

U.S. Vice President Richard B. Cheney grew up in Casper. Later, he served as Wyoming's U.S. congressman. When George W. Bush ran for U.S. president, he picked Cheney to be his running mate. They were elected in 2000 and 2004. Here, Cheney speaks to the state legislature in 2006.

the Senate and the House of Representatives. They meet each January, but only for forty days at most. People in Wyoming like to keep their government small.

Judicial Branch

Courts and judges make up the judicial branch. They may decide whether a person who is accused of committing a crime is guilty.

Local Government

Wyoming has twenty-three counties. Each county is governed by a group of three people known as a board of commissioners. Most cities and towns have a mayor and a city or town council.

WYOMING'S STATE GOVERNMENT

Executive		Legislative		Judicial	
Office	**Length of Term**	**Body**	**Length of Term**	**Court**	**Length of Term**
Governor	4 years	Senate (30 members)	4 years	Supreme (5 justices)	8 years
Secretary of State	4 years	House of Representatives (60 members)	2 years	Superior (19 judges)	6 years

Things to See and Do

Wyoming is a state with lots of room to move around. On the plains, in the mountains, and in the towns, you can find plenty to see and do.

Museums and Historical Sites

The state has many museums. Cheyenne Frontier Days Old West Museum is lots of fun. You can see old wagons, teepees, and much more there. Do you want to see the oldest building in Wyoming? It is at the Fort Laramie National Historic Site. You can tour this old trading post and fort. It is a good place to see how the fur traders and soldiers lived in the state's early days.

If you go to Cody, be sure to visit Old Trail Town. It is a famous ghost town and a wonderful place to learn about life in the Old West.

Riding, Roping, and Rhyming

Cowboys and poetry come together here! Cowboy poets write about their lives. Their poetry is about fixing fences, gathering cattle, and sitting around a campfire after a day's work. Some of these poets write about good horses, good friends, or the good old days. Cody, Jackson, Devils Tower, and other cities have cowboy poetry festivals each year.

The National Parks

Yellowstone was the first national park in the United States. Now, this Wyoming park is the nation's largest. Thousands of people go there to see grizzly bears, elk, and buffalo. They hike in the mountains and watch

Boiling water shoots out of the ground in Yellowstone National Park. Old Faithful erupts about once every eighty minutes.

Famous People of Wyoming

Jackson Pollock

Born: January 28, 1912, Cody, Wyoming

Died: August 12, 1956, East Hampton, New York

Jackson Pollock grew up in Wyoming loving art. In 1929, he moved to New York City to study painting. His paintings were often very large. To make a painting, he put a **canvas** on the floor and then poured and dripped paint on it in patterns. Some people said his paintings were not art at all. Pollock died at the age of forty-four in a car crash. Later, he was seen as an important artist. Today, his paintings are in many museums.

geysers shoot water high into the air.

Another popular spot is Grand Teton National Park. It is famous for its beautiful, snow-topped mountains. If you go there, you can hike, canoe, or watch for eagles, falcons, and other wildlife.

Sports

Lots of folks in Wyoming like rodeos. Cody holds a big rodeo in May. Cheyenne

Rodeos provide plenty of fast-paced fun in Wyoming. This steer roping contest is being held in Jackson.

has a famous rodeo in July. Smaller rodeos are held in towns across the state.

Wyoming is home to the Casper Rockies, a minor-league baseball team. Sports fans also follow their favorite high school and college teams. Hunting and fishing are popular with lots of people. In the winter, skiing and snowmobiling are great ways to enjoy the outdoors.

Famous People of Wyoming

Chris LeDoux

Born: October 2, 1948, Biloxi, Mississippi

Died: March 9, 2005, Casper, Wyoming

Chris LeDoux was a rodeo star and a well-known singer. He learned to ride horses on his grandfather's ranch. In high school, he became a bareback **bronc** riding champion. Later, he became a **professional** rodeo cowboy. He also played guitar and wrote and sang songs. LeDoux made about thirty albums. He sang with country music stars like Garth Brooks and Charlie Daniels.

Jackson Hole is famous for great skiing. The ski resorts around the town of Jackson have slopes for skiers of every skill level.

bronc — a horse that is still partly wild

campus — the land and buildings that belong to a college or university

canvas — cloth stretched over a wooden frame; used by artists for paintings

droughts — long periods of time without rain

fossils — bone or shell that has turned to stone over thousands of years

geysers — holes in the ground that allow steam and hot water to burst up

Great Depression — a time in the 1930s when many people lost jobs and businesses lost money

Great Plains — a huge area of mostly flat land in the center of the United States

immigrants — people who leave one country and move to another country to live

legislature — a group that makes laws

permanent — meant to last for a very long time

pioneers — the first people to settle in an area

professional — a person who earns a living doing a certain kind of work

reservation — land set apart by the government for a specific purpose

sacred — holy

strike — the stopping of work at a company by the workers who are trying to get better pay or working conditions

territory — an area that belongs to a country

Books

When Esther Morris Headed West: Women, Wyoming, and the Right to Vote. Connie Nordhielm Wooldridge (Holiday House)

Who'd Believe John Colter? Mary Blount Christian (Simon and Schuster Childrens Publishing)

Wyoming. Hello U.S.A. (series). Carlienne Frisch (Lerner Publishing Group)

Wyoming. One Nation (series). Patricia K. Kummer (Capstone Press)

Yellowstone National Park. David Petersen (Scholastic Library Publishing)

Web Sites

Enchanted Learning: Wyoming
www.enchantedlearning.com/usa/states/wyoming

Wyoming for Kids
www.wyoming4kids.org

Wyoming Government Site for Kids
www.wyoming.gov/kids.asp

Yellowstone National Park
www.nps.gov/yell/forkids/index.htm

INDEX